SOLVING MYSTERIES WITH SCIENCE

VAMPIRES AND WEREWOLVES

JANE BINGHAM

Raintree

Chicago, Illinois

Edited by Adam Miller, Vaarunika Dharmapala, and
Claire Throp
Designed by Ken Vail Graphic Design
Original illustrations © Capstone Global Library Ltd
2014
Illustrated by Chris King
Picture research by Mica Brancic
Production by Victoria Fitzgerald
Originated by Capstone Global Library Ltd
Printed and bound in China by CTPS

17 16 15 14 13
10 9 8 7 6 5 4 3 2 1

**Library of Congress Cataloging-in-Publication
Data**
Bingham, Jane.
  Vampires & werewolves / Jane Bingham.
    pages cm.—(Solving mysteries with science)
  Includes bibliographical references and index.
  ISBN 978-1-4109-5501-2 (hb)—ISBN 978-1-4109-
5507-4 (pb)
1. Vampires. 2. Werewolves. I. Title. II. Title:
Vampires and werewolves.

BF1556.B56 2013
133.4'23—dc23   2012042237

Acknowledgments
We would like to thank the following for permission
to reproduce photographs: © Mediscan p. 24;
akg-images p. 37 (Universal/Album); Alamy pp. 18
(© Mary Evans Picture Library), 21 (© Moviestore
collection Ltd), 38 (© INTERFOTO); Corbis p. 25
(epa/© STR); Flickr p. 34 left (Eddie); Fortean
Picture Library p. 33; Getty Images pp. 4 (Hulton
Archive), 5 (Universal), 20 (John Kobal Foundation),
22 (Evan Kafka), 23 (Stock Montage), 27 (American
International Pictures/Michael Ochs Archives), 28
(Art Wolfe), 29 (Archive Photos/Buyenlarge), 30
(Oxford Scientific), 31 (Photodisc/Darren Robb), 32
Archive Photos/George Eastman House), 35 (Hulton
Archive), 36 (Redferns/Fin Costello), 41 (Carsten
Koall), 43 bottom (NBce Universal/NBce/Syfy/Photo
by Philippe Bosse), 43 top (Hulton Archive/Moviepix/
Silver Screen Collection), 39; Science Photo Library
p. 40 (CCI Archives/J. M. G. Itard, Paris, 1801);
Shutterstock pp. 4 to 5, 15 (© Gualberto Becerra), 17
(© SOMMAI), 18 to 19 (© Albo003), 26 (© Kiselev
Andrey Valerevich), 34 right (© Dmitrijs Mihejevs),
38 to 39 (© Feraru Nicolae), 45 (© McCarthy's
PhotoWorks).

Background design images supplied by Shutterstock
(© C Salisbury), (© argus), (© Vitaly Korovin).

Cover photograph of a woman-witch reproduced with
permission of Shutterstock (© Arman Zhenikeyev)
and a veiled female vampire reproduced with
permission of Shutterstock (© Margaret M Stewart).

Every effort has been made to contact copyright
holders of material reproduced in this book. Any
omissions will be rectified in subsequent printings if
notice is given to the publisher.

Disclaimer
All the Internet addresses (URLs) given in this book
were valid at the time of going to press. However, due
to the dynamic nature of the Internet, some addresses
may have changed, or sites may have changed or
ceased to exist since publication. While the author
and publisher regret any inconvenience this may
cause readers, no responsibility for any such changes
can be accepted by either the author or the publisher.

CONTENTS

VAMPIRES AND WEREWOLVES: AN UNSOLVED MYSTERY

For centuries, people have told terrifying stories about vampires and werewolves. But what exactly are these mysterious creatures, and what makes them so frightening?

◀ The movie *Nosferatu* came out in 1922. Hundreds of vampire movies have been made since then.

What are vampires?

Vampires are featured in legends, art, books, and movies, and there are also many real-life accounts of vampire attacks. In some accounts, vampires are bat-like creatures with long, pointed fangs and leathery wings. Sometimes they are described as corpses that have risen from the grave, with claw-like fingernails and bloodshot eyes.

Some vampires look like ordinary humans, apart from their pointed upper teeth and their unusually pale skin. The one thing all vampires have in common is their thirst for human blood. They sink their fangs into their victims' throats and suck the blood from their veins.

What are werewolves?

Werewolves are terrifying creatures that are part-human and part-wolf. They usually stand upright, like a human, but they are covered with shaggy hair and have pointed ears and a snout like a wolf.

Werewolves let out bloodcurdling howls and snarls, and they have sharp teeth and claws to attack their victims. In many accounts of werewolves, men or women turn into werewolves for a short time and then regain their human form. This transformation usually happens at night, when there is a full moon.

▶ This spine-chilling image comes from the movie *A Vampire in London*, released in 1935.

Can the mystery be solved?

In the first part of this book, you can read some real-life stories of meetings with vampires and werewolves. The second part of the book asks the question: Can science solve the mystery of vampires and werewolves?

THE VILLAGE OF THE VAMPIRES

Back in the 1700s, the village of Meduegna was a sleepy place. Nothing exciting had ever happened in this quiet part of Eastern Europe. But then, in 1725, it became a scene of horror, fear, and dread...

As soon as Arnold Paole arrived in the village, people suspected that something was wrong. Why was he always so frightened, and why did he wake up screaming every night? Only his girlfriend knew the truth. Before he came to the village, Arnold had been attacked by a vampire, who had warned him that he would meet a horrible death. And it wasn't long before the warning came true. Arnold was working in the fields when he fell from a wagon and broke his neck.

MYSTERIOUS DEATHS

Arnold was buried in the village churchyard, but he did not stay quiet in his grave. Very soon, people were catching sight of him peering in at windows or knocking on doors. Everyone who saw him feared that he had come to drive them to their death—and they were right. In just a few weeks, four people had died mysteriously. The villagers decided it was time to take action.

HORROR IN THE GRAVEYARD

On a bright, moonlit night, five large men entered the churchyard. Working in silence, they dug up the newly buried coffin and pried open the lid...

The sight that met their eyes would haunt them forever. Instead of the pale, skinny young man whom they had buried, they saw a chubby figure with round, rosy cheeks. It was still Arnold, but now he looked as though he had been feasting for a month. The most terrifying sight of all was the trickle of scarlet blood running down his chin. They had unearthed a vampire!

DESTROYING THE VAMPIRE

The men staggered back in horror at the gruesome sight. They were desperate to run away, but they knew that they must stay and destroy the vampire. Otherwise, their village would never be safe again.

First, the priest stepped forward with his cross, hoping to terrify the evil creature. Then, another man raised a wooden stake above his head. Using all his strength, he plunged it deep into the vampire's chest.

...the priest stepped forward with his cross...

A STAKE THROUGH THE HEART

As the stake entered his heart, the vampire let out a horrible groan and blood came bursting out of the wound. It was a chilling sight, but at last the men could start to relax. The vampire was truly dead! But even then, their work was not yet over. First, they burned Arnold's corpse until they were sure there was nothing left of him. Then, they dug up the bodies of his victims and stabbed and burned them, to make sure they could never return as vampires. Finally, they scattered the graveyard with garlic, in order to keep other vampires away.

THE VAMPIRES RETURN!

The next five years passed peacefully in the village. But then the mysterious deaths began again. In a few short weeks, 11 people died, and not even the children were spared. This time, the villagers acted fast. A group of soldiers and doctors marched up to the graveyard and forced open all the coffins of the newly dead.

What they saw filled them with horror. All the corpses showed the same gruesome signs—swollen stomachs and faces and bloodstained mouths. The soldiers wasted no time in stabbing each body through the heart and burning the corpses. After this drastic action, there were no more unexplained deaths, but Meduegna became known and feared as the village of the vampires.

THE VAMPIRE IN THE CEMETERY

On a cold, dark night in March 1973, Sean Manchester squeezed through the railings of Highgate Cemetery in London, England. He was on a mission—to find and destroy an ancient vampire!

Centuries earlier, the body of a medieval lord, who had practiced black magic in Eastern Europe, had been buried in Highgate. And now he was on the prowl again!

HUNTING FOR THE VAMPIRE

Sean thought he knew exactly where to find the vampire. A few months earlier, a sleepwalking girl had led him to an enormous tomb with a gaping hole in the roof. Now he used a rope to let himself down into the dark, damp chamber.

Inside the tomb, Sean searched around for a body, but all he found was a cold, empty space. The vampire had escaped!

For the next three years, the vampire continued to roam the cemetery, and Sean continued his hunt, guided by the girl. In the end, she led him to the basement of an empty house. This time he found the vampire, stabbed it through the heart, and burned its body. The Highgate vampire was finally destroyed!

WEREWOLF ATTACK!

In the 1500s, life in the German town of Bedburg turned into a waking nightmare. It all began when some farmers found their animals lying dead in the fields. Cows, sheep, and goats had all been horribly slaughtered, with their limbs torn roughly from their bodies. The farmers blamed the wolves that lived in the nearby forest, and they built high fences to keep them out. But the mysterious slaughter continued. Then the horror grew much worse, as the unknown killer turned to human victims...

FEAR AND HORROR

Over the next few months, the town was gripped with panic. Children disappeared from their homes and young women vanished on their way to work. Some were found dead, with their bodies ripped apart. Others simply disappeared without a trace. Meanwhile, several people had glimpsed a tall, wolf-like figure running for the woods. Could a werewolf be preying upon their town?

The terrible mystery remained unsolved, until one morning, when a group of children was playing in a meadow. Suddenly, a terrifying creature leapt from the bushes. He was covered in thick, shaggy hair and had a face like a ferocious wolf. He raced toward the children with a terrifying howl and seized a little girl by the throat.

IN THE GRIP OF A WEREWOLF

The girl felt the werewolf's fingers tighten around her throat, and she was prepared to die a terrible death. But then she felt him losing his grip. She had been saved by the stiff white collar that her mother always made her wear! She wriggled out of his grasp and ran for her life.

A TERRIBLE SECRET

Once the little girl was safely home, she described her attacker, saying: "He looked really scary—half like a man and half like a wolf. But the weirdest thing about him was his eyes. I'm sure I've seen those eyes somewhere before!"

Everyone was puzzled by her words—except Peter Stumpp. He was a middle-aged farmer who was well respected in the town. But he had a terrible secret. Only he knew the truth about the werewolf.

A SHOCKING DISCOVERY

After the girl's lucky escape, there were more mysterious deaths. It seemed that the horror would never end, until at last a massive hunt was planned. A crowd of men and dogs headed for the forest, where they spotted a wolf-like creature running through the trees. The dogs raced after the creature, and after a long, hard chase, they managed to pin it down. But when the men arrived on the scene, they were amazed.

Instead of the savage wolf they had expected, there was a man lying on the ground. It was Peter Stumpp, someone they had always believed to be their friend.

A MAGIC BELT

Stumpp was imprisoned and tried for the murder of 13 women and children. At his trial, he told an astonishing story. He said that the devil had given him a magic belt that had the power to turn him into a wolf. Sometimes, Peter admitted, he felt a powerful urge to put on the belt. Then he stopped being his usual, gentle self and became a savage killer instead.

Stumpp was found guilty of murder and was burned to death. Some people said that he had invented the story of the magic belt as a way to prove his innocence. Others believed that he really could turn into a werewolf. But whatever the truth may be, people have never forgotten the werewolf of Bedburg.

THE BEAST OF BRAY ROAD

Is it possible that a savage werewolf could be living somewhere in the United States today? Some people believe that a strange beast lurks on Bray Road, near Elkhorn, Wisconsin—and they have some terrifying stories to prove it.

CHASED BY A BEAST

On the evening of October 31, 1999, Doristine Gipson was driving along Bray Road when she felt her car tires hit something on the road. Stepping out of her car, she peered into the darkness. At first, the road seemed clear, but then she saw a tall, hairy figure racing toward her. It was at least six feet tall, with enormous hands and feet. Terrified, she jumped into the driver's seat, but before she could get away, the beast took a flying leap and landed on her car.

A LUCKY ESCAPE

Trying her best not to scream, Doristine slammed her foot down hard on the accelerator. The car took off with a sudden lurch, and the beast fell back onto the road with a sickening thump. Doristine headed home as fast as she could. The next day she told her neighbors about her scary meeting with a mysterious wolf-like creature.

STRANGE MEETINGS

As the news spread, more and more people came up with their own stories of a sinister creature that was spotted near Bray Road. A girl had been terrified by an enormous dog that walked on its hind legs. A farmer had chased a tall, hairy beast that had suddenly disappeared, leaving a set of massive footprints. A woman in a car had seen a kneeling figure with a wolf's head. She was convinced that it was a werewolf and described its pointed ears, glittering yellow eyes, and long, wolf-like snout.

No one has ever explained these scary sights. Even today, there are still reports of a mysterious beast prowling the area. Is it any wonder that drivers on Bray Road feel very uneasy after dark?

INVESTIGATING VAMPIRES AND WEREWOLVES

What is the truth behind the stories of vampires and werewolves? Many people have tried to find explanations for the legends and real-life accounts. In this part of the book, you can read about these theories. You can also discover how the theories stand up to the test of science and common sense.

ANCIENT LEGENDS

People have told stories about savage, bloodsucking creatures for thousands of years, although these creatures were not always known as vampires and werewolves. The people of ancient Syria, Persia, India, and China all had legends of supernatural spirits that visited humans by night and drank their blood. They also told stories of humans who could turn into wild creatures. These ancient legends were adapted by the Hebrew people, the ancient Greeks, and the Romans, and belief in vampires and werewolves spread throughout Europe during the Middle Ages. Stories of vampires and werewolves were especially popular in parts of Eastern Europe, such as Serbia and Romania. These countries were covered with thick, dark forests. So it was easy for people to imagine that all sorts of frightening creatures lived in the depths of the forests.

▼ The legend of a vampire preying on an innocent young woman is found in many cultures.

A scientific approach

Wherever possible, this book will use the scientific method in order to unravel the mystery of vampires and werewolves. You can learn more about the scientific method in the box below.

THE SCIENTIFIC METHOD

Good investigators follow the scientific method when they need to establish and test a theory. The scientific method has five basic steps:

1. Make observations (comments based on studying something closely).

2. Do some background research.

3. Form a testable hypothesis. This is basically a prediction, or "educated guess," to explain the observations.

4. Conduct experiments or find evidence to support the hypothesis.

5. After thinking carefully about the evidence, draw conclusions.

Ask question

Do background research

Construct hypothesis

Test with an experiment

Analyze results. Draw conclusion

Think! Try again.

Hypothesis is true

Hypothesis is false or partially true

Report results

Count Dracula

Until the 20th century, legends of vampires were not well known outside Eastern Europe. But vampire stories spread rapidly after 1897, when the Irish writer Bram Stoker published *Dracula*.

The hero of the novel is Count Dracula, a handsome nobleman who is also a vampire. Dracula lives in a castle in the remote kingdom of Transylvania, in Eastern Europe, and lures his victims to their deaths. The character of Count Dracula was based on a real 15th-century prince, Vlad the Impaler (see page 38), but Dracula in the novel also has supernatural powers. The dramatic figure of Count Dracula had a huge impact on people's imaginations. He has appeared in movies, TV series, and even cartoons.

▼ The image of Count Dracula as elegant and wealthy became very popular in the 1930s.

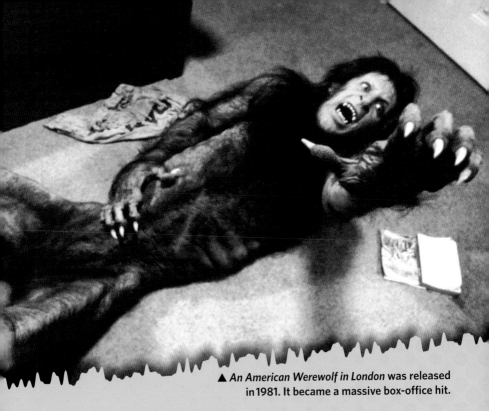

▲ *An American Werewolf in London* was released in 1981. It became a massive box-office hit.

Modern vampires and werewolves

Vampires and werewolves have starred in hundreds of horror movies. They have also inspired some popular series for teenagers. In *Buffy the Vampire Slayer*, a teenage girl battles against vampires. The *Twilight* novels and movies feature a 100-year-old vampire named Edward Cullen and a werewolf named Jacob Black. The Harry Potter novels and movies also include vampires and werewolves. Remus Lupin, a professor at Hogwarts School, is a werewolf.

KILLING VAMPIRES AND WEREWOLVES

Vampires and werewolves are very hard to destroy, but there are some methods that are believed to work. According to the legends, you can kill a vampire by stabbing it through the heart with a wooden stake, and a werewolf will die if you shoot it with a silver bullet. Both vampires and werewolves are afraid of sunlight or anything made of silver, while vampires also fear iron, running water, and their own reflections. Vampires are terrified of the sight of a Christian cross and can be driven away by garlic.

STRANGE SYMPTOMS

Is it possible that some accounts of meetings with vampires and werewolves were in fact encounters with people? This chapter will examine this theory. It will ask whether some vampires and werewolves were real people who looked unusual or who behaved strangely as a result of a disease or a medical condition.

Rabies

Were some people who were feared as vampires really suffering from rabies? Rabies is a disease that affects the brain, causing victims to become extremely violent. Sufferers from rabies may roll on the ground, eat dirt, foam at the mouth, and attack anyone in sight. Rabies is caught from dogs and other mammals that bite their victims, and human sufferers sometimes bite other people. They also become extremely sensitive to light and develop a fear of water—just like the vampires in stories!

▶ A dog infected with rabies is a terrifying sight—and humans with the disease are even more frightening.

Studying the evidence

Today, rabies has been almost entirely wiped out, but it was widespread at the time when many of the vampire stories were told. Juan Gomez-Alonso, a Spanish neurologist (expert in diseases of the brain), has studied the evidence carefully. He concludes that an outbreak of rabies was the cause of a wave of vampire-like behavior in Serbia in the 1700s, at the time of the case of Arnold Paole (see pages 6 to 9).

▶ Vlad the Impaler was the model for Bram Stoker's Count Dracula (see page 20). It is believed that he suffered from porphyria (see below).

Porphyria: The "vampire disease"

Some vampire stories may have been triggered by cases of porphyria in a community. This is a rare blood disease that can be inherited, but is not infectious. People with porphyria have reddish teeth and lips and purple-colored urine. Their teeth protrude (stick out) from their gums and they are extremely sensitive to light. They also behave in a violent way, with sudden twitches and jerks. Until the 20th century, anyone with this range of symptoms would have been greatly feared by others in their community, and people may have made up horror stories about them.

Porphyria and vampires

In 1985, Dr. David Dolphin, a Canadian biochemist, suggested that there could be a link between stories of vampires and cases of porphyria. He considered all the symptoms of porphyria and compared them to descriptions of vampires in traditional legends. Dolphin also noted that part of the modern cure for porphyria is a course of injections of healthy blood. He claimed that it was possible that sufferers in the past discovered that they felt better if they consumed other people's blood. However, Dolphin admitted that more research was needed to support his theory.

Porphyria and werewolves

Some scientists believe that cases of porphyria can also be linked to werewolf legends. If people with porphyria are exposed to sunlight, blisters form on their skin, and these blisters can sprout fine hair as they heal. People with porphyria often have increased hair growth on their forehead, and their hands can become deformed and paw-like as a result of blistering. Is it possible that uneducated villagers saw these unusual-looking people and feared that they were not entirely human?

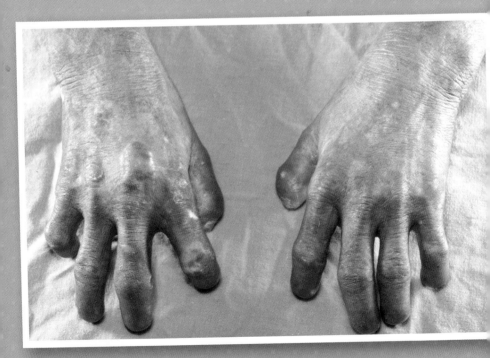

▲ If porphyria is untreated, sufferers can develop severely deformed hands. To people with no understanding of medical science, these hands could seem like a monster's paws.

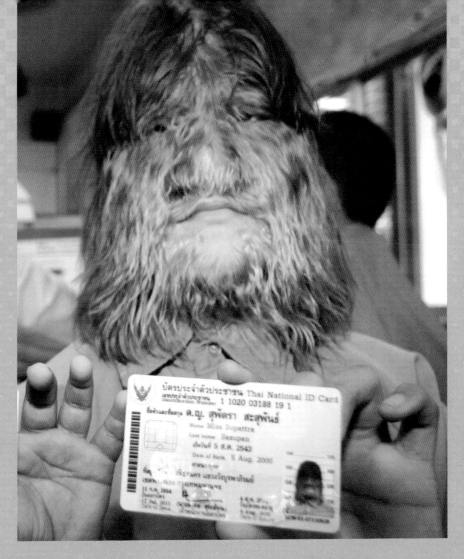

▲ This photo shows a girl with hypertrichosis. This inherited condition is found in a tiny number of families.

Hypertrichosis

The medical condition of hypertrichosis can make people look a bit like werewolves. Hypertrichosis is a very rare condition that usually runs in families. People with hypertrichosis grow large amounts of long, thick hair. In some cases, the hair covers the whole body. In other cases, just the face is affected.

In the past, people with hypertrichosis would have been greatly feared. They may even have been driven from their communities and forced to hide in nearby forests. It is possible that these unusually hairy people were believed to be werewolves.

Dead or undead?

Many vampire stories include an account of digging up the corpse of a suspected vampire. In tales like the "village of the vampires" (see pages 6–9), the villagers discover a corpse with a rounded stomach, rosy cheeks, and traces of blood around its mouth. All these signs are interpreted as clear evidence that the vampire is "undead." The villagers are convinced that the vampire is rising from its grave to feast on the blood of the living. But can this deduction stand up to the test of science?

Signs of life?

After a body has been buried for a few weeks, it starts to decompose (decay) and produce gases. This natural process of decay produces the same signs that are described in vampire stories. The corpse fills up with gases that make it seem fatter than before. The gases under the skin also make the skin look pinker and smoother than it did when the person was alive. If a body is disturbed, a dark liquid flows out of its mouth. This liquid looks very much like blood.

Myth-buster

Groans or gas?

Most vampire stories describe the dramatic moment of a vampire's death, when the creature is stabbed through the heart and lets out a loud groan. But is this evidence that the vampire had been alive? In fact, science can explain the groaning noise. A decomposing body is full of trapped gas. When the body is pierced, the gas escapes with a loud exploding sound, similar to a human groan.

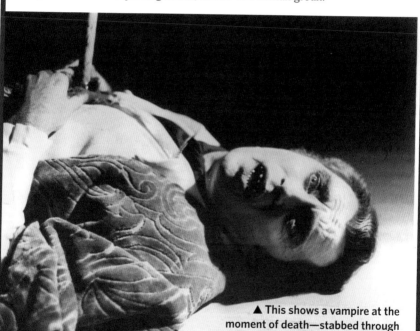

▲ This shows a vampire at the moment of death—stabbed through the heart with a wooden stake.

CREATURES OF THE NIGHT

Many stories of vampires and werewolves date from a time when people lived in fear of wild animals. People were especially fearful at night, when they could only partly see what was attacking them. It is likely that some accounts of vampires or werewolves were based on meetings with real nocturnal (nighttime) creatures. It is also possible that sightings of vampires and werewolves were in fact hallucinations—images of things that were not really there. This chapter looks at the evidence for these theories.

Wolves or werewolves?

Until the 1900s, packs of wolves roamed through the forests of Europe, and they could be heard howling loudly at night. Wolves often made nighttime raids on villages, leaving animals dead and wounded. Wolves usually attack at night, so there were very few witnesses. After an attack, there would be reports of a terrifying creature with a shaggy body, glittering eyes, and enormous fangs. Sometimes the reports described a creature that stood up on its hind legs. It is not surprising that stories grew up about werewolves—terrifying wolf-like creatures that were as clever as human beings.

◀ The howl of a wolf at night is a truly spine-chilling sound.

Wolf-men

In some ancient societies, hunters and warriors dressed in wolfskins for their ceremonies and dances. So maybe these wolf-like figures helped to create the legend of the werewolf? People may have feared that the dancers could turn into wolves and attack them.

▲ The Cheyennes wear wolfskins for traditional dances.

DIFFERENT HUNTERS

It is possible that some people confused wolves with werewolves. But wolves hunt in a different way than the werewolves in stories. Wolves usually hunt in packs, unlike the solitary werewolf. It is also very unusual for a wolf to kill a human being.

Vampires and bats

Could some vampire legends have been inspired by people's fear of bats? In many stories, the vampires look like bats, with pointed fangs and huge, leathery wings. Vampires sink their fangs into a victim's neck to suck their blood—the same frightening method of hunting that is practiced by bloodsucking bats. There are three species of bats that feed on blood, and they all use their sharp fangs to pierce the neck of an animal, such as a pig.

▼ This bat is feasting on the blood of a pig. Bloodsucking bats are usually known as vampire bats.

Myth-buster

Bloodsuckers—or not?

Most vampire legends have their origins in Eastern Europe. However, the bats of Europe are not bloodsuckers, so the idea of bloodsucking vampires does not come from bats. Bloodsucking bats are only found in Central America and South America.

Shadowy creatures

Could it be that some people's experiences of vampires and werewolves are based on nothing more than scary shadows? Scientists have conducted experiments to discover how the human brain responds to shadows. They have found that the brain turns shadowy shapes into images that it recognizes. It is very common for shadows and other vague shapes to be interpreted as a cloaked figure or as a scary creature, such as a wolf or a bat. So it is quite possible that people could mistake shadowy shapes for vampires and werewolves.

▲ Many people are scared of bats and their spooky-looking shadows.

VISIONS OF VAMPIRES

It is possible that some reports of vampires came from witnesses who were losing their sight. When people are almost blind, they experience some very vivid hallucinations. This is because their brains have to work overtime to create an image from very little visual information. People who are losing their sight often describe seeing a grotesque face with prominent teeth, like a vampire. You can read more about this effect on page 45.

FEAR AND SUPERSTITION

Stories of vampires and werewolves reflect a fear of the supernatural and the unexplained. This chapter will examine some of the fears and superstitions that lie behind beliefs in vampires and werewolves. It will also put the superstitions to the test of science and common sense.

▶ When a baby died suddenly, people often tried to find a supernatural cause for the tragic death.

Someone to blame

Before the 20th century, people had a limited understanding of illness and disease. Healthy adults and children would become sick and die for no apparent reason, and plagues would suddenly sweep through a community. People wanted someone to blame for these disasters, so they told stories of vampires and werewolves that preyed on innocent victims. Sometimes people identified a particular person as a vampire or a werewolf. Then that person became a scapegoat—someone who could be blamed for the sudden deaths in their community (see the story of Mercy Brown on pages 34–35).

THE VAMPIRE IN THE CRADLE

People have always been horrified by the sudden death of a baby and have tried to find a cause for the tragedy. In the past, there was a widespread belief that vampires preyed on babies in their cradles and sucked their blood while they lay sleeping. People placed iron objects under a baby's cradle, in the hope that they would scare away any vampires.

◀ The chupacabra is a mythical monster thought to exist in parts of Latin America, where it supposedly sucks the blood of animals, particularly goats.

BELIEFS TODAY

Even in the 21st century, fears about vampires and werewolves have not completely died out. In 2002, rumors of vampires swept through villages in Malawi, in southern Africa. One group of villagers even beat a man to death based on the suspicion that he was sucking their blood. In 2004, villagers in Marotinu de Sus, Romania, dug up the corpse of Petre Toma, a suspected vampire, and burned his heart.

▲ The grave of Mercy Brown can still be seen in Exeter, Rhode Island.

Mercy Brown— vampire or victim?

Until the 20th century, belief in vampires was widespread in many parts of North America. This belief led to some dramatic events in Rhode Island in the early 1890s. The problem began when four members of the Brown family became very sick. They all grew pale, weak, and breathless and they coughed up blood. The mother was the first to die, followed by the eldest daughter. Two years later, a son became very ill, and the following year, a daughter, Mercy, became sick and died.

Death by vampire?

Faced with this series of mysterious deaths, the local community looked around for a cause. They concluded that one member of the family must be preying on the others. A group of neighbors, including Mercy's father, dug up the bodies of the three dead women to look for signs that they were "undead." The most recently buried was 19-year-old Mercy, and it was decided that she was to blame for the deaths. Her body was removed from its tomb and her heart was cut out and burned. But, despite these actions, her brother died soon afterward.

A medical explanation

Later, an investigation revealed a simple cause for the deaths. All four members of the Brown family had died from tuberculosis. Tuberculosis is a very serious lung disease that is easily passed from one person to another if they are living closely together. Symptoms of the disease include extreme paleness, weakness, and bleeding from the mouth. It is easy to understand how people with little medical knowledge could draw the wrong conclusions from these signs. To them, the symptoms of tuberculosis appeared to be evidence that a vampire was preying on the family.

VARNEY THE VAMPYRE; OR, THE FEAST OF BLOOD.

FLORA ENCOUNTERS VARNEY IN THE SUMMER-HOUSE.

◀ Belief in vampires was widespread at the time of the case of Mercy Brown. This page comes from a popular 19th-century story, *Varney the Vampire, or the Feast of Blood.*

CHAPTER XXXIV.

THE THREAT.—ITS CONSEQUENCES.—THE RESCUE, AND SIR FRANCIS VARNEY'S DANGER.

SIR FRANCIS VARNEY now paused again, and he seemed for a few moments to gloat over the helpless condition of her whom he had so determined to make his victim; there was no look of pity in his face, no one touch of human kind-

ness could be found in the whole expression of those diabolical features; and he delayed making the attempt to strike into the heart of that unhappy, but beautiful being, it could not be from any merciful feeling, but simply, that he wished, during a few moments to indulge his imagination with the idea of perfecting his villainy effectually.

Alas! and they who would have flown to her rescue,—they, who for her sake have chanced all accidents, ay, even death itself, were sleeping, and knew not of their loved one's danger. She was alone—far enough from the house, to be drawn to that tottering verge where sanity ends and the dream of madness, with all its terrors commences.

But still she slept—if that half-

Shape-shifting

In some stories and legends, an ordinary man or woman is transformed into a vampire or a werewolf. Sometimes this transformation is permanent. But often people shift between their everyday, human self and their darker self as a vampire or a werewolf. This change from one state to another is especially common in werewolf legends. In many werewolf legends, a human turns into a werewolf at the time of the full moon. Some stories, such as the Werewolf of Bedburg (see pages 12–15), feature a magic belt that a man puts on and is suddenly transformed into a werewolf.

▼ Werewolves are especially frightening because they resemble a crazy human being as well as a wolf.

Magic or science?

In the past, people blamed black magic for the
transformation of an ordinary person into a vampire
or a werewolf. But was the change really caused by
magic? Many people experience sudden changes in
mood and behavior, and these changes can often be
explained by medical science.

Mental illness

Mental illness can produce dramatic changes in
personality. In particular, people with schizophrenia
move rapidly from one mental state to another.
Schizophrenics can have long periods when they
behave in a completely calm and rational (reasonable)
way, but they can also have times when they become
violent and disturbed. In these psychotic periods,
they may hear voices telling them to perform violent
acts. People with bipolar disorder can also experience
dramatic changes in mood and behavior if their
condition is not treated carefully.

Before the discovery of drugs to control mental illness,
people would have experienced some very distressing
symptoms. It is possible that others in their community
would have looked for ways to explain the changes in
the people they knew.

REAL VAMPIRES AND WEREWOLVES?

Are there real people who behave like vampires or werewolves? This chapter will take a look at some examples from the past and in the present day.

Vlad the Impaler

In the 1400s, Prince Vlad Tepes Dracula lived in a remote castle in the kingdom of Transylvania, in Eastern Europe. He earned the nickname "Vlad the Impaler" because of his gruesome habit for impaling (spearing) his enemies on wooden stakes. Vlad is believed to have killed over 80,000 victims, and his reputation for cruelty spread throughout Europe. He became even more famous after Bram Stoker used him as the model for Count Dracula in his novel *Dracula* (see page 20).

▶ **This horrific scene shows Vlad the Impaler with some of his victims. Vlad was incredibly cruel, but there is no evidence that he drank human blood.**

A cruel countess

Countess Elizabeth Báthory came from Hungary, where she lived from 1560 to 1614. She was terrified of growing old and became convinced that bathing in fresh blood was the secret to staying young. It is believed that she tortured and killed hundreds of people, mostly young women. Elizabeth kept a diary of her killings, but it is not known whether she drank the blood of her victims.

◄ Elizabeth Báthory believed she could stay young and beautiful if she bathed every day in human blood.

Drinking blood

There have been several cases of murderers who behaved like vampires, drinking their victims' blood. These deranged killers include the German Peter Kürten, who was tried in the 1930s, and the American Richard Chase, who was sent to prison in 1979. Journalists who reported on these trials claimed that the killers were suffering from Renfield's syndrome. This condition was named after Dracula's assistant in Bram Stoker's novel *Dracula*. People with Renfield's syndrome believe that they are vampires and have a very strong urge to drink blood. Renfield's syndrome is sometimes known as clinical vampirism, but most doctors do not recognize it as a real illness.

Acting like wolves

Lycanthropy is a rare mental illness that makes people act like wolves—or werewolves. Sufferers from lycanthropy believe that they have turned into a wolf. They develop wolf-like behavior, such as snarling and howling. It is possible that Peter Stumpp (see pages 12–15) was suffering from lycanthropy.

RAISED BY WOLVES

There have been cases of children who were abandoned or lost in a forest and were raised by wolves. In the 1700s, the wolf-boy of Aveyron, in southern France, lived with wolves until he was around 12 years old. His hair hung over his eyes, his body was filthy and covered with scars, and he usually walked on all fours. The boy communicated by howling and snarling and tore at his food with his teeth.

▶ This portrait of Victor, the wolf boy of Aveyron, was made after he had been captured and cleaned up. He never managed to live like a normal boy.

Living like wolves

Throughout history, there have been men and women who have chosen to hide away from other people and live like animals. These feral (wild) humans usually live in woods or forests and survive by gathering food and hunting. Feral men and women were especially common in the Middle Ages, when people who had broken the law lived as outlaws in the forest.

After many years of living in the wild, a person can appear to be like a wild animal, such as a wolf. It is possible that a meeting with a feral man or woman was the trigger for some of the werewolf stories.

DRESSING UP

Some people choose to dress like vampires. These people, who are often known as goths, dress mainly in black and wear very pale makeup, with lots of black eyeliner and red or purple lipstick. A few "vampire goths" even file their teeth to make them look like pointed fangs! Although goths might like to look like vampires, they do not perform cruel or violent acts. It is just for fun!

▲ Goths like to look scary, but they don't behave like vampires!

CAN THE MYSTERY BE SOLVED?

People have feared vampires and werewolves for thousands of years. Even today, our fear of these mysterious creatures is kept alive in movies, books, and TV programs. But is there a scientific explanation for vampires and werewolves?

All sorts of theories

There are many theories about the nature and origins of vampires and werewolves. Some experts claim that the legends were based on real people who were suffering from medical conditions, such as rabies, porphyria, or hypertrichosis. Other experts argue that the scary figures of the undead were in fact corpses that had begun to decay.

It has been claimed that tales of vampires and werewolves may result from a deep-seated fear of wolves and bats. And some stories may have been triggered by scary shadows or by hallucinations.

There may also be a social explanation for vampires and werewolves. Were these hated creatures simply people who behaved in an unusual way, and who were made into scapegoats for any unexplained deaths in their community?

Looking at the evidence

As you look at all the different theories, consider the evidence carefully. Did people at the time really understand what they saw? Were they influenced by fear and superstition? And what was the social background to the stories of vampires and werewolves? All these factors need to be taken into account before you draw your conclusions.

▶ The idea that a man can become a werewolf remains very strong today. In the TV series *Being Human*, the character of Josh turns into a werewolf.

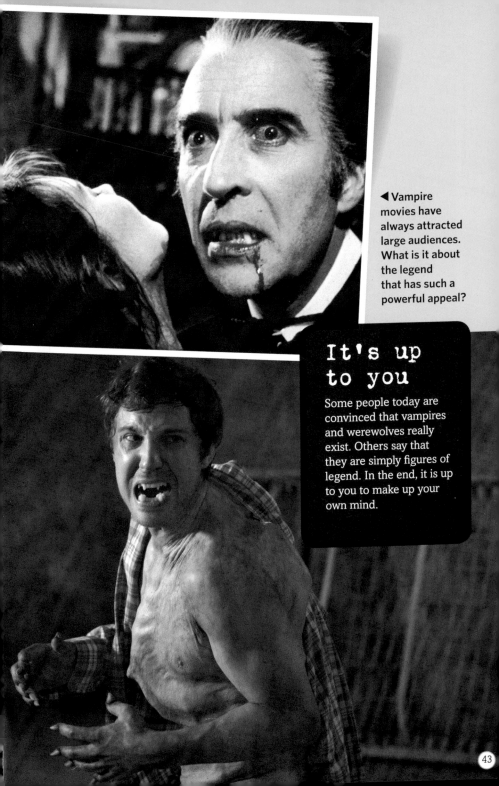

◀ Vampire movies have always attracted large audiences. What is it about the legend that has such a powerful appeal?

It's up to you

Some people today are convinced that vampires and werewolves really exist. Others say that they are simply figures of legend. In the end, it is up to you to make up your own mind.

TIMELINE

c.1000 BCE
People in many parts of the world tell stories of bloodsucking creatures and savage wolf-men. These legends are adapted by the Hebrews, the ancient Greeks, and the Romans.

1476 CE
Vlad the Impaler dies in Transylvania

1588
The female Werewolf of Auvergne, in central France, is tried and burned at the stake

1589
Peter Stumpp is tried and burned as a werewolf in Bedburg, Germany

1614
Countess Elizabeth Báthory dies in Hungary

1700s
Fear of vampires starts to sweep through Eastern Europe

1725
Arnold Paole is condemned as a vampire in Meduegna, Serbia. Peter Plogojowitz is condemned as a vampire in Serbia in the same year.

1764
The Beast of Gévaudan, in southern France, begins three years of killings

1892
Mercy Brown is condemned as a vampire in Rhode Island

1897
Bram Stoker publishes *Dracula*

1931
The Hungarian actor Bela Lugosi stars in the movie *Dracula*, wearing elegant evening clothes

1935
The movie *Werewolf of London* is released

1973
Sean Manchester leads a vampire hunt in Highgate Cemetery, in London

1981
The movie *An American Werewolf in London* is released

1992
The movie *Bram Stoker's Dracula*, directed by Francis Ford Coppola, is released

1997
The first episode of *Buffy the Vampire Slayer* is shown on television

1999
Doristine Gipson is chased by the beast of Bray Road in Elkhorn, Wisconsin

2004
Villagers in Marotinu de Sus, Romania, dig up the corpse of a suspected vampire

2005
Stephenie Meyer publishes the first book in her vampire romance series, *Twilight*

2008
The movie *Twilight* is released

2011
The movie *Breaking Dawn* is released. It is the fourth in the *Twilight* movie series.

SUMMING UP THE SCIENCE

It has been claimed that people who are going blind experience hallucinations of a grotesque face, similar to a vampire (see page 31). But what is the science behind this claim?

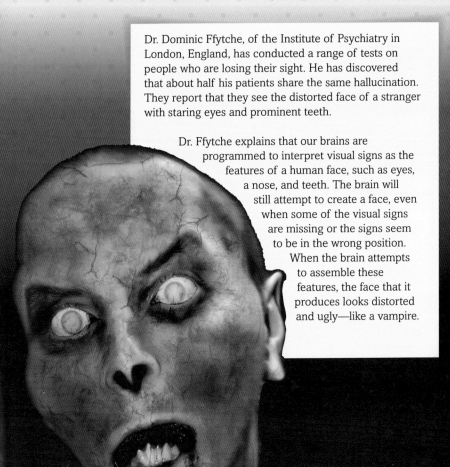

Dr. Dominic Ffytche, of the Institute of Psychiatry in London, England, has conducted a range of tests on people who are losing their sight. He has discovered that about half his patients share the same hallucination. They report that they see the distorted face of a stranger with staring eyes and prominent teeth.

Dr. Ffytche explains that our brains are programmed to interpret visual signs as the features of a human face, such as eyes, a nose, and teeth. The brain will still attempt to create a face, even when some of the visual signs are missing or the signs seem to be in the wrong position. When the brain attempts to assemble these features, the face that it produces looks distorted and ugly—like a vampire.

GLOSSARY

adapt change or remake in some way

biochemist scientist who studies biology and chemistry

bipolar disorder mental illness that causes dramatic mood changes

condition health problem

corpse dead body

deduction decision made after thinking hard about the evidence

deformed changed from a normal shape and appearance

deranged crazy or insane

distorted changed from a normal shape

encounter meeting

fangs long, pointed teeth

feral living like a wild animal

hallucination image that appears to be real, but does not in fact exist

infectious spread from one person to another by germs in the air or by physical contact

inherited passed on from parents to their children

lure encourage someone to do something

medieval dating from the period between the 5th and 15th centuries

programmed trained to do a certain job

prominent sticking out

psychotic out of control and out of touch with reality

rabies medical condition that causes some mammals, including people, to act in a violent way, foam at the mouth, and become very sensitive to light

schizophrenia severe mental illness that causes people to have hallucinations, psychotic behavior, and rapid changes of mood

snout nose and mouth of an animal such as a wolf, dog, or pig

supernatural beyond the natural world

symptom sign of illness

transformation change

tried found guilty in a court of law

undead dead, but still appearing to have a living body

FIND OUT MORE

Books

Allen, Judy. *Fantasy Encyclopedia*. Boston: Kingfisher, 2005.

De'Ath, Otto. *The Vampire Hunter's Guide* (Monster Tracker). Mankato, Minn.: Sea-to-Sea, 2012.

Ganeri, Anita. *Vampires and the Undead* (Dark Side). New York: PowerKids, 2011.

Ganeri, Anita. *Werewolves and Other Shapeshifters* (Dark Side). New York: PowerKids, 2011.

Lestrade, Ursula. *The Werewolf Hunter's Guide* (Monster Tracker). Mankato, Minn.: Sea-to-Sea, 2012.

Regan, Lisa. *Vampires, Werewolves and Zombies*. New York: Tangerine, 2009.

Web sites

www.crystalinks.com/vampires.html
This illustrated guide to vampires includes a history of vampires in different cultures.

www.hp-lexicon.org/bestiary/bestiary_v.html
This site has information about vampires in the Harry Potter novels.

www.hp-lexicon.org/bestiary/werewolves.html
Find out more about werewolves and their links to the Harry Potter novels.

Topics to research

- Folk tales and legends of vampires and werewolves
- Vampires and werewolves in movies, TV, and books
- Victor of Aveyron, known as the "Wolf Boy."

INDEX